Aretha Franklin

by Jillian Carroll

Chicago, Illinois

© 2004 Raintree
Published by Raintree, a division of Reed Elsevier, Inc.
Chicago, Illinois
Customer Service: 888-363-4266
Visit our website at www.raintreelibrary.com

For information, address the publisher
Raintree, 100 N. LaSalle, Suite 1200, Chicago, IL 60602

Printed and bound in the United States at Lake Book Manufacturing, Inc.
07 06 05 04 03
10 9 8 7 6 5 4 3 2 1

Library of Congress Cataloging-in-Publication Data:

Carroll, Jillian.
  Aretha Franklin / Jillian Carroll.
     v. cm. -- (African-American biographies)
Includes bibliographical references (p.   ) and index.
Contents: The Queen of soul -- Gospel roots -- On the road -- Voice of a
movement -- Stardom -- Peaks and valleys -- Back in the groove -- Diva
at last.
  ISBN 0-7398-7029-7 (library binding-hardcover) -- ISBN 1-4109-0314-1
(pbk.)
  1. Franklin, Aretha--Juvenile literature 2. Singers--United
States--Biography--Juvenile literature. 3. African American
singers--Biography--Juvenile literature. [1. Franklin, Aretha. 2.
Singers. 3. Soul music. 4. African Americans--Biography. 5.
Women--Biography.] I. Title. II. Series: African American biographies
(Chicago, Ill.)
  ML3930.F68C36 2003
  782.421644'092--dc20

                          2003001510

Acknowledgments
The publishers would like to thank the following for permission to reproduce photographs:
pp. 4, 21, 32, 38, 48 Bettmann/Corbis; pp. 6, 10, 18, 22, 26, 36 Library of Congress; p. 8 Corbis; pp. 14, 24 Hulton/Archive by Getty Images; p. 30 Hulton-Deutsch Collection/Corbis; p. 35 Neal Preston/Corbis; pp. 41, 44 Roger Ressmeyer/Corbis; pp. 47, 55, 58 Associated Press, AP; p. 52 Corbis Sygma; p. 56 Reuters NewMedia Inc./Corbis.

Cover photograph: Hulton-Deutsch Collection/Corbis

Some words are shown in bold, **like this.** You can find out what they mean by looking in the glossary.

Contents

Known as the Queen of Soul, Aretha Franklin shaped American music with a variety of musical styles and a voice that touches peoples' hearts. Here she poses for a photograph in 1968 at the height of her career.

Introduction

Aretha Franklin has dazzled music fans for more than 45 years. She started singing **gospel** in her father's church when she was twelve years old. Gospel music combines traditional church songs with African-American musical styles. Aretha also became a talented **rhythm and blues (R & B)**, singer. **Blues** music is a type of emotional music created by African slaves in America. It comes from the slaves calling to each other across the fields as they worked. R & B mixes this sad sound with African-American folk music and a strong beat. But Aretha did not stop there. She blended gospel and R & B into a whole new sound. Listeners called this blend **soul.**

Aretha has an amazing voice. This musical gift has made her one of America's top female singers. Her range amazes listeners. Her voice can soar to the highest note at the top of the scale. It can slide down to a growl. The New York Times called her voice "one of the glories of American music." She is known as the Queen of Soul.

Many African Americans protested unfair treatment in the 1950s and 1960s. Most called for an end to segregation.

Aretha began her career during a time of segregation in the United States. **Segregation** was the separation of blacks and whites according to law. Blacks and whites were separated in schools, restaurants, washrooms, and many other places. Segregation created a **color bar,** or an imaginary boundary that made it nearly impossible for black people to achieve success. It seemed as though the color barrier applied to music as well. Musical artists made music for blacks or for whites. They did not make music for both. Aretha was one of the first musicians to cross that barrier. Her music appealed to millions of listeners, no matter what the color of their skin.

Even after more than 40 year of music making, Aretha continues to dazzle. In 1999 the music television station VH1 honored her. On their list of the "100 Greatest Women of Rock and Roll," Aretha was named number one.

In her own words

"I look for a good **lyric,** a good melody, something meaningful. When I go into the studio I put everything into it. Even the kitchen sink."

"I'm a very versatile vocalist. That's what I think a singer should be. Whatever it is, I can sing it."

There were many cotton fields in the South in the early and mid-1900s. Some African Americans, including Reverend Franklin, worked in these fields picking cotton.

Chapter 1:
Gospel Roots

Aretha Louise Franklin was born March 25, 1942, in Memphis, Tennessee. She was born just months after the United States entered World War II (1939–1945). She was the fourth of five children born to the Reverend Clarence Franklin and Barbara Siggers Franklin. Her parents named her after two of her father's sisters, Aretha and Louise.

Reverend Franklin was a handsome minister with a booming voice and a gift for drama. He spent his early years picking cotton under the hot Mississippi sun. He came from a family of **sharecroppers.** This meant they raised crops, but they had to share them with the landowner. They did not own the land and they were poor. But Franklin refused to let poverty destroy his dreams. He worked hard and got an education. His talent and love of God led him to become a minister.

Many African Americans joined or worked for the National Association for the Advancement of Colored People (NAACP) during the Civil Rights Era. The NAACP was started in 1907.

Aretha's parents met in Mississippi and then moved to Memphis. Reverend Franklin ministered and preached at Memphis's New Salem Baptist Church when Aretha was born. To preach means to give a religious talk to people. Aretha was still a baby when the family moved to Buffalo, New York. There, both of her parents worked at the Friendship Baptist Church. Barbara Franklin helped with the music. On Sundays her clear, powerful voice filled the church with traditional **gospel** songs. On weekdays she worked as a nurse's aide.

Moving to Motown

The Franklin family moved to Detroit, Michigan, when Aretha was two. In the 1940s, Detroit was a growing city that was full of opportunity. Many Detroit factories were making weapons for World War II. There were also a lot of automobile factories. The city had so many car factories that people nicknamed Detroit the Motor City or "Motown." Thousands of African Americans from the South moved north to Detroit to begin a new life. The North was not as **segregated** as the South.

The Franklin family soon became very involved with the New Bethel Baptist Church. Every Sunday, Reverend Franklin energetically preached to members of the 4,500-seat church. Reverend Franklin had a talent for preaching. People around the country would later say Reverend Franklin had a million-dollar voice. The New Bethel **congregation** was one of the first to hear it. A congregation is a group of people gathered together for prayer. Later, other congregations around the country invited Reverend Franklin to preach at their churches. He went on to become one of the first ministers to record his sermons.

Reverend and Barbara Franklin separated when Aretha was six. Barbara Franklin moved back to Buffalo. She and Reverend Franklin agreed that the children should stay in Detroit during the school year. In the summer, they would live with their mother. Aretha phoned and wrote to her mother during the rest of the year.

In 1952 Barbara Franklin had a heart attack and died. Aretha's visits to Buffalo became a treasured memory.

Music everywhere

Aretha missed her mother's lovely voice. Yet the Franklin home continued to be filled with music. Reverend Franklin knew many musicians. Many of these musicians stayed with the Franklins when they were in town. There were two pianos, a radio, and a record player in the large house. Aretha remembers times when all were in use at the same time. She and her sisters, Erma and Carolyn, took piano lessons. Aretha did not want to take piano lessons. She would hide in the coat closet when her piano teacher came to the house. She thought the practice exercises were dull. She wanted to play songs.

Aretha never learned to read music. That means she never learned to look at a sheet of music and play from it. Instead, she learned to play songs by listening to them. **Gospel** singer and composer Reverend James Cleveland was among the many guests who stopped at the Franklin home. He taught Aretha some basic piano chords. Her talent took her from there. She began playing and singing songs she had heard on the radio for her father's guests. Reverend Franklin quickly realized his daughter had special musical talents. Aretha was singing solos at New Bethel by the time she was twelve.

Mahalia Jackson

Mahalia Jackson brought the sounds of gospel music to a worldwide audience. She was born in New Orleans in 1911. She grew up listening to **jazz** and singing in local churches. When Mahalia was sixteen, she moved to Chicago, where she opened a beauty parlor. In the 1930s, she began recording albums and toured with a gospel group. In 1946 her recording of "Move On Up a Little Higher" sold more than two million copies. It drew the attention of the nation and earned her the nickname "The Gospel Queen." By 1954 she had her own radio and television programs. Jackson supported the **Civil Rights Movement**. The Civil Rights Movement was the struggle to gain full citizenship rights for African Americans. Many African Americans and whites supported the movement to give all people the same civil rights. In 1963 Jackson sang at the Civil Rights Movements' March on Washington in Washington, D.C. Jackson died in 1972.

The 1950s have been called the golden age of gospel music. Gospel groups traveled across the country to sing at churches and clubs. Some of these groups visited the Franklin home when they were in town. Aretha loved the visitors. Her skill as a singer improved rapidly with help from powerful singers such as Mahalia Jackson. Aretha's taste in music also expanded. She loved the sounds of the **R & B** and the jazz she heard on the radio. Jazz is lively music, started by African Americans, that is full of rhythm. Aretha decided she wanted to be a professional singer.

Aretha smiles for a studio portrait for Columbia Records in 1960, shortly after signing a five year contract with the record company.

Chapter 2: On the Road

Reverend Franklin worked hard on his preaching. He recorded some of the inspiring sermons he gave at New Bethel. Eventually, he would record more than 60 albums. It was not long before African-American **congregations** around the country were asking him to visit.

Aretha went on tour with her father. They drove from town to town and from church to church. Restaurants and hotels were **segregated** then. Aretha recalls driving between shows and passing many roadside restaurants. However, they were for whites only. The Franklins had to drive into cities and towns to find restaurants where African Americans could eat.

On tour, Reverend Franklin would preach while his daughter accompanied him on the piano. She was surprisingly good on the piano even though she had not taken many lessons. Later, Aretha also sang. Her music and her father's preaching often brought audiences to tears and shouts.

First record

Chess Records had recorded the Reverend Franklin's sermons. Now, they asked him if they could record his daughter. He agreed, and Aretha made her first record in 1956. It was a live album of nine **gospel** songs. Her voice was so strong that few people would have guessed the singer was still a teenager.

In the late 1950s, gospel music gave way to pop, or popular, music. One of Aretha's childhood friends had already moved into pop music. His name was Sam Cooke, and he was a well-known gospel singer. But now Sam Cooke's smooth voice could be heard on popular radio stations. Now Aretha did not want to sing only gospel. She especially admired **jazz** and **blues** singer Dinah Washington. She, too, had visited the Franklin home in Detroit. Aretha began to think about singing something other than gospel.

A contract and a husband

In 1960 Aretha moved to New York City. She was 18. She took singing and dancing lessons and hired a manager. Soon after she arrived, Aretha signed a five-year contract with Columbia Records. Her first album was called *The Great Aretha Franklin.* But both the album and her contract were disappointing. The people at Columbia did not seem to know what to do with Aretha's powerful voice. They wanted to make Aretha a jazz singer. But that was not the style of music Aretha sang best. She couldn't dazzle audiences with her jazz the way she could with her gospel and blues. Some of the songs from that first album were played on the radio, but none of the songs were big hits. The album did not make her a star.

Aretha often returned to Detroit to visit her family. On one of these trips, in 1961, she met Ted White. White was a manager for musicians. He took over managing Aretha's career and they began to date. White asked her to marry him six months after they met. They married while they were on tour. Aretha and Ted lived in Detroit when they were not touring.

The Civil Rights Movement

Around this time, some big changes were taking place across the United States. Many African Americans had begun actively campaigning for their **civil rights** in the mid-1950s. Civil rights are the rights of all citizens to fair and equal treatment under the law. African Americans were tired of being treated unfairly and unequally. Both African Americans and whites were holding protests, marches, and **boycotts.** To boycott means to refuse to buy or take part in something as a way of protest. They were trying to change the nation's laws and attitudes.

One of the leaders of the **Civil Rights Movement** was the Reverend Dr. Martin Luther King Jr. King had a way with words. He inspired many black, and some white, people to protest **racism** and

Dr. Martin Luther King Jr.

Dr. Martin Luther King Jr. was born in 1929 in Atlanta, Georgia. His father was a minister. Dr. King decided to be a minister too. In college, King learned about the work of an Indian man named Mohandas Gandhi. Gandhi used nonviolent protests to gain India's independence from England. Years later, Dr King was minister at an African-American church in Montgomery, Alabama. One of his church members, Rosa Parks, was arrested for refusing to give up her bus seat to a white person. Her decision led Dr. King to ask for a nonviolent protest of the kind that Gandhi had led. He asked people to **boycott** the buses. The city eventually agreed to treat African Americans and whites equally on its buses.

Dr. King made many enemies through his work. Many people did not want African Americans to have **equal rights**. Dr. King was shot to death by one of those enemies in 1968. Aretha sang at his funeral.

segregation. Racism is the practice of the belief that one race is better than another. King gathered people together for nonviolent protests. He asked for all people of all colors to live together peacefully.

In 1963 King spoke at a **civil rights** march in Detroit that Reverend Franklin helped organize. Later, King spoke at the March on Washington in the nation's capital. He gave a speech called "I Have A Dream" about his desire for peace and equality among all people. This famous speech is now considered one of history's most important. More than 250,000 people traveled to Washington for the march. Many famous musicians, including Mahalia Jackson, performed there.

The Chitlin Circuit

Aretha toured constantly during her first years with Columbia. She sang **R & B** and **jazz** at shabby nightclubs, hotels, and small concert halls. Her audiences were almost entirely African-American. People called these all-black clubs the **Chitlin Circuit.** Aretha was often uncomfortable in these clubs and halls. They were not always in safe neighborhoods. And she struggled with shyness and stage fright during her early years of performing. She finally got over it by imagining that the audience members were friends of hers.

She also developed a **reputation** for being difficult to work with during those years. A reputation is what other people have heard about a person. It might have been because she wasn't singing the music she wanted to be singing. Columbia wanted Aretha to be a jazz-pop star. But her voice was meant for something different.

By now, Aretha was an experienced and well-known **jazz** singer. She toured in the Caribbean. She performed at the Newport Jazz Festival. This is a famous jazz festival that attracts people from around the world.

In 1963 Dinah Washington died suddenly. Aretha knew her as an old family friend as well as an amazing musician. Ms. Washington's death inspired Aretha to record an album in memory of her. On *Unforgettable,* she sang one of Washington's R & B songs called "Soulville." Music critics consider *Unforgettable* Aretha's best work from her Columbia days.

On to Atlantic

By 1966 Aretha had recorded a dozen disappointing albums with Columbia. She and White had added a son, Teddy Jr., to their family. Aretha's contract with Columbia was finished. White decided that a change was in order. So Aretha signed a contract with Atlantic Records. At the time, Atlantic was a small, independent record label. It focused on African-American music, such as **R & B, blues,** and **jazz.**

Aretha's **producer** at Atlantic Records was a white man named Jerry Wexler. A producer is a person in charge of making a record. Wexler let Aretha choose her own songs and **arrange** them. To arrange music means to change a piece someone else has performed so it can be played on different instruments, or in

Throughout her career, Aretha has frequently posed for publicity photos such as this one.

a different way. She had never been able to work that way at Columbia. The producers at Columbia had chosen the songs Aretha sang and decided how she would sing them. She had no say in the recording process at all. But at Atlantic, she wrote some of her own songs. She played the keyboards. She even used her sisters, Erma and Carolyn, as her backup singers. Wexler put it all together. Soon, the hits started coming.

Many English rock and roll groups, such as the Beatles, as well as Elvis Presley in the United States, said African-American music was an inspiration for their sound.

Finding Her Voice

Aretha's first **single** with Atlantic was the 1967 hit "I Never Loved a Man (the Way I Love You)." Radio stations could not play the song often enough. Listeners could not seem to hear it often enough. This was mainly because of a change that had begun in the late 1950s. Record players and radios began to play a new sound. It had rhythm and used electric guitar, and it was called rock and roll. African Americans knew that the rock and roll sound was not new. It was their sound. But it only became popular with white audiences when white musicians began playing it. On top of that, English bands like the Beatles and the Rolling Stones were becoming extremely popular around the world. These English bands always gave credit to the African-American music that had inspired their sound.

By the mid-1960s, white audiences were used to hearing rock and roll. They wanted to hear more different kinds of music. White audiences in the United States started listening to music from African-American performers. They listened to **R & B** and **jazz.**

Aretha had found a large audience. She had also found her voice. She now sang with more power and confidence. Suddenly, Aretha was a big star. Billboard magazine named her the top female vocalist of 1967. Her **single** sold more than a million copies. It was included on a record Atlantic released later that year. That album, also called *I Never Loved a Man the Way I Love You,* sold 250,000 copies in two weeks. Soon it went gold. An album is certified gold when it sells 500,000 copies.

I Never Loved a Man the Way I Love You included five songs that became hit singles. One of them was a song called "Respect." "Respect" was written by Otis Redding. He was one of the most popular performers of R & B music in the 1960s. Sadly, he died in a plane crash when he was only 26 years old.

During a time of racial and political unrest, Aretha's songs helped shape a movement for equality. Here, Aretha poses for an Atlantic Records label photo shoot in 1968.

Chapter 3:
Voice of a Movement

By 1967 the United States was a very different place from the United States of Aretha's childhood. African Americans were united against **segregation**. Laws that treated African Americans unfairly had been changed. But in many ways, African Americans still did not have equal opportunities. The attitudes of many white people had not changed. **Racism** was still a problem. It was hard for African Americans to get an education, a good job, or a decent place to live. Change was a slow process.

Some African Americans thought the change was too slow. This slowness made them angry, and led to **race riots** in major cities. Race riots were outbreaks of violence between blacks and whites. They happened mainly in inner-city neighborhoods. African-American rioters stole things and burned homes, buildings, and businesses. The riots showed the anger and hopelessness many African Americans living in these poor neighborhoods felt.

Women were also fighting for their rights in the 1960s. Betty Friedan was the president of the National Organization of Women (NOW) in 1967. She and many others worked to help get women's rights written into law.

African Americans were not the only people fighting for **equal rights** in the 1960s. Women were also struggling for their rights. Women were not allowed to do many things that men could do. Instead, they were encouraged only to be wives and mothers. They were not encouraged to be scientists, business leaders, doctors, or lawyers. They were told to be pretty and nice, but they were not told to be smart or strong. In the 1960s, many women began asking why this was so. They demanded that women be allowed the right to be whatever they wanted.

A new sound

The time was right for Aretha's unique brand of music, and the 1967 Grammy Awards took notice. The Grammy Awards are an annual event to honor the best recorded music of the year. Originally, the Grammys had only one category for **R & B** recordings. It was an award for best R & B recording. But Aretha had had 10 hits in the last eighteen months. Her popularity and the popularity of R & B led to more awards for that kind of music. Aretha won the 1967 Grammy Awards for Best R & B Recording and Best R & B Performance, Female. She won the Grammy for Best R & B Performance, Female, eight years in a row. People began calling it the Aretha Franklin Award. In total, Aretha has won fifteen Grammy Awards. That is more than any other female artist.

On a roll of hits

Aretha followed up her first Atlantic album with *Aretha Arrives*. She had a special challenge recording that album. She had recently had fallen off a concert stage and shattered her right elbow. Her elbow was in a cast. She had to play the album's piano parts with her left hand only.

Aretha Arrives had songs from a wide variety of musical styles. But Aretha had no problem switching between the styles. She did a song by the rock group the Rolling Stones, and a smooth song made famous by Frank Sinatra, a pop singer. It was a surprising mix, but it worked.

Respect

Aretha's audiences continue to ask that she perform "Respect." Even today, it is a song that many people can relate to. In the 1960s, however, the song seemed to mean even more.

The United States was in uproar in 1967. There was a lot of anger between the races, and between men and women. African Americans turned the song "Respect" into a battle cry for the **Civil Rights Movement.** At the same time, women were demanding respect from men. They are people, too, African Americans and women said, and as people, they deserve respect.

Aretha's "Respect" was a song that was perfect for its time. Because of the movements of the time, millions of people related to the song. Aretha turned "Respect" into solid gold. The smash hit went on to become her trademark song, or the song she is best known for.

In 1968, Aretha made *Lady Soul.* It included the smash hit "Chain of Fools" and sold 1 million copies. The record also included "(You Make Me Feel Like) A Natural Woman." Since "Respect," her popularity continued to grow. Through that song, Aretha had become an important symbol of both **civil rights** and women's rights.

The queen and Dr. King

In 1968 the mayor of Detroit declared February 16 to be Aretha Franklin Day. He did it to honor the famous singer's many accomplishments. Aretha gave a concert in Detroit that evening. It was her first sold-out concert.

During the concert, Dr. Martin Luther King Jr. joined her on stage. Aretha had known Dr. King since she was a little girl. He was a friend of her father. That night, King gave her a special award from the Southern Christian Leadership Conference. This was a group of black churches and ministers that guided the Civil Rights Movement. Aretha had performed at several marches and protests to help the movement and support King. To acknowledge this, he gave her an honorary civil rights award.

Dr. King had always loved **gospel** music. He often asked Aretha to sing "Precious Lord." In April of 1968, Dr. King was shot and killed. Aretha choked back her tears to sing "Precious Lord" at his funeral.

With a handful of hit songs climbing the charts, Aretha has reason to be happy in this 1968 photo.

Chapter 4:
Stardom

Aretha began her first European tour immediately after Dr. King's death in the spring of 1968. She spent two weeks visiting major cities in five European countries. Aretha received great reviews. She sang at the famous Olympia Theater in Paris, France. At first, Aretha was puzzled by the audience's response. They were very quiet. Aretha had never sung to such a quiet audience. She was afraid they were not enjoying themselves. The audience did not stand and clap until the end of the concert. But then they would not stop clapping. Aretha learned that most French people save their applause for the end of any performance.

Aretha made a live album from her Olympia performance called *Aretha in Paris*. It was one of three albums she recorded in 1968. In those days, artists were expected to put out a new album every five or six months. Today, popular artists may wait three to four years or more between albums.

On August 27, 1968, Aretha sang a soul version of the National Anthem. This began the second session of the Democratic National Convention.

Not all the songs on Aretha's albums were new. She would record a mix of original and **cover** songs. Covers are songs originally recorded by other performers. Aretha has covered songs by many different artists throughout her career. She has performed songs by Jimi Hendrix, the Beatles, and Elton John. She moves easily between **blues, rhythm & blues (R & B)**, pop, rock, **gospel,** and other musical styles.

Aretha brought her own style of singing to the songs she covered. Her one-time band mate, sax player King Curtis, believed Aretha was one of the very best performers ever. In his opinion no one would ever be able to sing or perform a particular song better than Aretha.

Life of a star

The **Civil Rights Movement** was coming to an end. But Aretha remained a visible symbol of the advances made by African Americans. In August of 1968, Aretha was part of an important event. She sang a **soul** version of the national anthem at the Democratic Party's national convention. National conventions are held every four years. Members of the main political parties gather at these conventions to choose their candidate for president. A political party is a group of people who have similar views about how a country's government should be run. Aretha's performance at this convention sent a strong message. It said that African Americans were becoming a full part of the nation's political and musical life.

By the end of 1968, Aretha was a true star. Her last few albums had all gone to the top of the charts. Her success led her to work with other famous musicians. Atlantic paired Aretha with stars like Eric Clapton and Cissy Houston. Cissy Houston was a famous gospel singer. She also sang backup vocals for Elvis Presley. Aretha and Houston had worked together at Columbia. At Atlantic, Houston and her group the Sweet Inspirations became Aretha's new backup singers. Sometimes, Houston's daughter attended the recording sessions. Her name was Whitney. She called Aretha "Aunt Ree." Years later Whitney Houston would recall watching Aunt Ree and her mother sing together.

Aretha's life was now a blur of concerts, interviews, and time squeezed in with family. *Time* magazine did a cover story on her after her European tour. But the article upset rather than pleased Aretha. She thought the writer had not gotten the facts right. The experience left a bad taste in Aretha's mouth. She refused to give journalists any interviews for years afterward.

Aretha put out three more albums in 1969, including *Soul '69*. Despite its name, *Soul '69* was actually a **blues** and **jazz** album. But it was not the light, poppy jazz she had recorded for Columbia. This jazz was heavy, full of harmony, and performed by a full orchestra. Aretha sounded relaxed and welcoming on the album. Her voice was full of feeling and emotion. She sang songs that called attention to this amazing voice and ability. She had never sounded better.

Aretha's career was at its peak. But her marriage was falling apart. Aretha became very sad and she began to eat a lot for comfort. She gained weight. She used to perform in tight gowns decorated with lots of sequins. Now Aretha wore loose, flowing dresses to hide

Aretha performed with backup singers on the television show Soul Train *in the early 1970s. By then Aretha was already known as the Queen of Soul.*

the extra pounds. Her sadness caused her to cancel some concerts and recording sessions. She and Ted White divorced in 1969.

A new life, a new look

Aretha took some time off from recording to deal with her divorce. Then she returned to the studio to make her first album of the 1970s. It was called *This Girl's in Love with You.*

Ray Charles

Ray Charles has been called one of the most important **blues** musicians of the twentieth century. He was born in Albany, Georgia, in 1930. He lost his eyesight as a child and studied music and piano at a special school for the blind. He left school at age fifteen to start his own trio. He had his first hit, "Georgia on My Mind," in 1960. Since then, he has become famous for his blend of country blues, **jazz**, and **gospel** music. He is also known for his emotional **soul** singing and excellent piano playing.

Aretha found a new love in the 1970s. Ken Cunningham was a businessman. The two made a home together in New York City. Aretha had her fourth son, Kecalf (pronounced "Celf"), with Cunningham. Kecalf stood for "Ken E. Cunningham/Aretha Louise Franklin."

It was time for Aretha to go back on the road. A lot had changed since her last tour. The largest audiences for live music now were young rock and roll fans. Aretha had to change with the times, too. Fortunately, she was up to the challenge.

The new Aretha Franklin was bolder and different than she had been. Aretha had always performed in elaborate wigs and gowns. Now, she styled her hair in an Afro and wore short, simple dresses. She applied her own style when she covered popular songs, such as "Bridge over Troubled Water," a song by Simon and Garfunkel. She also recorded a live album in 1971. It was called *Aretha Live at the Fillmore West*.

Live at the Fillmore West

San Francisco's Fillmore West concert hall had hosted some of the biggest names in rock and roll. It did not have chairs or bleachers. The audience sat on the floor or stood during the performances. Wexler booked Aretha at the Fillmore West to make a live album. He wanted to make the Queen of Soul a rock star.

Aretha amazed rock-and-roll fans for three sold-out shows at the Fillmore West. She sang her trademark **soul** songs, including "Respect." She also sang pop hits that were still high on the charts. Soul legend Ray Charles joined her for the final night. All of it went on the album *Aretha Live at the Fillmore West*. The recording was certified gold. Aretha had successfully performed soul hits for rock and roll fans. She had connected with a whole new audience.

Aretha received so many Grammy Awards for Best R & B Performance, Female, that some people referred to the award as the Aretha Franklin Award. Here she is shown accepting one of the awards in March 1972.

Chapter 5:
Peaks and Valleys

Like the 1960s, the 1970s was a time of big change. African Americans had begun to make some gains from their struggle for **equal rights**. Many began to take more pride in their heritage, and Aretha was among them. Her next album, *Young, Gifted, and Black,* made it clear that Aretha was proud to be an African American. The album featured five more hit **singles**.

Aretha's next project was a risky one. She was no longer known as a **gospel** singer. But Wexler had long wanted Aretha to record another gospel album. She finally agreed.

It was another live album. For two nights, Aretha performed and recorded at a church in Los Angeles, California. Her father even preached during the recording session. *Amazing Grace* was released in 1972. It became the best-selling **gospel** album up to that time. Aretha received credit as the album's co-**producer.** It even won Aretha another Grammy Award.

Aretha's next album came out in 1973. It was the first of many disappointments. Aretha's sister Carolyn wrote the album's only hit, "Angel." It became Aretha's thirteenth number-one hit on the R & B chart. But Aretha would have just one more top-ten pop hit in the 1970s.

Disappointments

Aretha's personal life, on the other hand, was going well. She was happy in her relationship with Cunningham. They traveled to the Caribbean and Europe together. She had lost nearly 40 pounds in the early 1970s. Her decision to lose weight occurred when she went into a dress shop. The clerk began showing her size-fifteen clothes. Aretha decided then and there to lose weight. She got into such good shape she began to add dancing to her performances.

Aretha was in a period of artistic struggle. The American music scene was changing. People used to like **soul, rhythm & blues (R & B)**, and ballads. Ballads are slow songs that tell a story. Now musical tastes were changing. People wanted to hear a fast-paced dance music called disco. Aretha did not want to abandon rock, soul, and R & B for disco. But it was not a good time to make and sell these kinds of records.

Aretha, her husband Glynn Turman, and her son, Kecalf, relax at their new home in Encino, California, in 1981.

Wexler left Atlantic in 1975. Aretha struggled to find a producer with whom she could make more magic. In 1976 a new and different opportunity presented itself. Aretha was asked to make the soundtrack, or music, for a movie. *Sparkle* was about three young African-American women. They were trying to become a successful singing trio. Aretha did an R & B album of the songs for the movie. It was a success although it was filled with a style of music that was fading in popularity. The *Sparkle* album became Aretha's first gold album in three years.

Her personal life was now hurting, however. Aretha had gained back much of the weight she had lost and was not in very good shape. She also began having problems with Cunningham. The two thought a change of scenery might help their relationship. They decided to move to Los Angeles. Many other musicians had already made the move from the East to the West Coast. Aretha, Cunningham, and her children moved into a home in Encino, California. But Aretha and Cunningham separated soon afterward. Cunningham returned to New York.

Changes

Aretha was very comfortable in her new home. She loved to spend time there gardening, cooking, and parenting her boys. Her four sons were showing their own musical abilities. Eventually, her son Teddy would play guitar in his mother's band. Her son Clarence would write songs. Clarence also introduced Aretha to her next husband.

It happened when Aretha appeared at a benefit for needy children. She was in her dressing room while Clarence collected autographs from stars at the benefit. Clarence was introduced to actor Glynn Turman. Turman had starred in several television shows, including *What's Happening,* a popular sitcom in the late 1970s. "My mother just loves you," Clarence told the actor. "Who's your mother?" asked Turman. Clarence took Turman to Aretha's dressing room. That was in January 1977. Aretha and Turman were engaged by the end of the year. In Detroit the following April, Aretha's father married them in his church.

In the summer of 1979, Aretha received some bad news. Burglars had broken into her father's home in Detroit. He was shot during the robbery. Although he was still alive, he was unconscious. Unconscious people are not awake and are not able to see, think, or feel. The Reverend Clarence Franklin remained unconscious until his death five years later, in 1984. Aretha never heard his booming voice again.

In 1980 Aretha signed a contract with Arista Records. She also took a role in the movie *The Blues Brothers.* She played a restaurant owner who is upset with her musician husband. Her husband wants to leave her to join the Blues Brothers Band. Aretha wore a stained pink waitress outfit and bedroom slippers for the role. She started singing her 1968 hit "Think" when her husband announced he was leaving. She liked making the movie, and her performance drew good reviews

In 1981 Aretha played the piano for Clive Davis. Davis founded Arista Records in 1974.

Chapter 6:
Back in the Groove

In the early 1980s, Aretha split her time between California and staying at her father's side in Detroit. It was a very difficult time. Aretha had never liked flying. Now she had to fly more than ever.

She was also worried about money. She had made a lot of money throughout her career. But she never was able to manage it well. Aretha's friends say she does not trust people outside her family. They say she prefers to handle her own business affairs. But Aretha is sometimes too busy to pay bills on time. And she loves giving money away to charities and to people in need. She likes spending money on clothes, home, friends, and family. Not surprisingly, she found herself short on cash in the early 1980s.

Aretha turned to her new partners at Arista Records for help. She hoped the record label could help put new life into her career.

On track at Arista

Aretha stopped in London during one of her first tours with Arista. There, she sang for Prince Charles and the Queen Mother. The event reminded Aretha of something her father had once said. He had told her that one day she would sing for kings and queens. Aretha felt sad to think that her father would not know that his words had come true.

Reverend Franklin's condition put a strain on Aretha's marriage. In 1982 Aretha moved back to the Detroit area to be with her father. Turman stayed in Los Angeles. Aretha knew that it would be hard on their marriage to be so far from each other. However, she was relieved to be back in the Detroit area. Turman and Aretha divorced in 1984.

Over the following years, Aretha sang with many very famous performers such Elton John, James Brown, and others. In 1985 she starred in her first music video for the hit "Freeway of Love." She reached out to younger audiences, recording a duet with a popular singer named George Michael. She also sang with Keith Richards and Ron Wood of the Rolling Stones. The three did a **cover** of the Rolling Stones' song "Jumpin' Jack Flash," for a movie of the same name. Actor Whoopi Goldberg was the star of the movie. She played one of the backup singers in the song's video.

Aretha sings a duet with James Brown at the Taboo nightclub in Detroit, Michigan on January 11, 1987.

Back in church

In 1986 politicians in Michigan declared Aretha's voice one of the state's greatest natural resources. A natural resource is a material found in nature that is useful to people. The politicians were telling Aretha that her voice was an incredible natural beauty.

Aretha began experiencing real success in her career again. She planned a project that would take her back to her **gospel** roots

Aretha has performed at the inaugurations of two U.S. presidents. In January of 1993, she sang in front of the Lincoln Memorial at President Bill Clinton's inauguration.

one more time. Fans had been asking her to sing **gospel** music ever since *Amazing Grace.* So Aretha decided to record a gospel album in her father's church and in his memory.

Aretha recorded *One Lord, One Faith, One Baptism* in three nights in 1987. Like *Amazing Grace,* it had the feeling of a church service with a lot more music. Aretha's brother Cecil recited a prayer, and Aretha and her sisters sang some of their favorite gospel songs. *One Lord, One Faith, One Baptism* won two Grammy Awards.

In 1987 Aretha made history. She became the first woman in the Rock and Roll Hall of Fame. The hall honors people who have made rock and roll music an important part of America.

A string of painful deaths began in 1988. That year, Aretha's sister Carolyn died of cancer in April. Then her brother Cecil died of cancer in 1989. The following year, Aretha lost her grandmother. Aretha asked her remaining brother, Vaughn, to go on the road with her. She asked him to help her manage her business. He agreed.

Honors and awards

The two of them were soon on their way to Washington, D.C. The newly elected President Bill Clinton was a big fan of Aretha's. She was asked to sing at his inauguration celebration in 1993. An inauguration is the ceremony that begins the term of a president or other public official. Aretha had sung in 1977 for President Jimmy Carter's inauguration, too. This time, she shared the stage with the pop-rock band Fleetwood Mac.

A year later, Aretha returned to Washington, D.C., to accept another honor. She became the youngest person ever to receive a Kennedy Center Honor. Kennedy Center Honors recognize the nation's best artists. At the award ceremony, performers sang to her for a change. In Los Angeles that same year, the Grammy Awards gave Aretha a Lifetime Achievement Award. It recognized all that Aretha had done for music.

She made all of these trips by bus. Aretha stopped flying in the mid-1980s after she had a bad experience on a small plane. Beginning in 1984, she recorded all her albums in Detroit. Her fear of flying put some limits on what Aretha could do. But she did not let that stop her. She has told interviewers that she prefers her fancy tour bus to any plane. In a bus, she said, she can pull over anytime. She cannot do that in a plane.

Name that tune

Africans who were sold into slavery in the United States brought their music with them. These slaves would greatly inspire musicians of all races. Slaves sang spirituals to help them through long, hard working days. Spirituals were songs of prayer and praise. Slaves also used these songs to communicate with each other. The song's **lyrics** held secrets known only to them.

Blues developed directly from spirituals. A group of singers typically sang a spiritual. Blues were emotional, sometimes sad, songs sung by one person. They did not have to be about religion. Like spirituals, though, singers had the freedom to change the words and melodies if they liked.

Black **gospel** music became popular in the 1930s. The style began with the traditional church songs. Black musicians mixed them with spirituals and added African-American rhythms.

Jazz has roots in blues and other African-influenced forms of music. Jazz music has lively rhythms, and the musicians often improvise, or

Aretha loves food. Losing weight has been one of the biggest challenges of her life. Another was quitting smoking. She finally managed to quit in 1991. Quitting greatly improved the sound and range of her voice.

make up the music, as they play. Jazz is considered the first truly American music form.

Rhythm and blues (R & B) combines rural blues with the danceable rhythms found in some jazz music. It developed in the 1940s. When white musicians such as Elvis Presley began playing R & B–influenced music with more guitar in the 1950s, it was called rock and roll.

Soul combines elements of gospel, jazz, and rhythm and blues. Songs tend to be slow and are sung with a lot of feeling.

Funk is a type of bass-heavy dance music that is focused on jazz rhythms. Like jazz, it is often improvised. It was developed by artists such as James Brown and George Clinton in the 1960s and 1970s.

Rap music began in the late 1970s. Rhythmic, urban poetry is spoken, or rapped, over funky, or funk inspired, beats. **Hip-hop** music uses rap-like beats but isn't necessarily rapped to. It tends to be more danceable than rap, and is typically a mixture of rap, pop, and R & B.

In 1998 Aretha was asked to make her second appearance in a movie. Aretha likes the moviemaking process and is shown here on the set of the movie The Blues Brothers 2000.

Chapter 7:
Diva at Last

A retha showed no sign of slowing down as the end of the century approached. She signed a contract to write a book about the story of her life. She started her own film production company and record label. She was accepted to the famous Julliard School in New York to study classical piano.

In 1998 she had a role in the *Blues Brothers 2000 movie.* She played the same character as before, but sang a different song. She treated *Blues Brothers 2000* audiences to a new version of "Respect." Aretha said she never gets tired of singing "Respect." It does not matter that she has been singing it for more than thirty years.

Aretha also released a new album in 1998. It was called *A Rose Is Still a Rose.* Pop singer Lauryn Hill wrote the album's title track. Aretha's recording of it hit both the **R & B** and pop music charts. It was Aretha's first album in seven years. It showed her sound had changed with the times, though. There was even a **hip-hop** influence in some of the songs. That modern sound further opened people's eyes to Aretha's talent.

Opera singer

Aretha had a special chance to show the range of her talents at the 1997 Grammy Awards. Opera legend Luciano Pavarotti had been scheduled to sing at the awards. Opera is a play in which all or most of the words are sung and the singer is accompanied by an orchestra. The Grammy's producers came running to Aretha just fifteen minutes before Pavarotti was to perform. They told her he was too ill to sing during the live broadcast. They asked if Aretha could sing the aria he had been going to perform. An aria is elaborate song performed by a single singer. Absolutely, she said, She said yes even though opera is very different from the kind of music she usually sang.

Aretha had sung a version of the song just once before. She had no time to practice. She quickly listened to a recording of it. Minutes later, she sang it in front of 1.5 billion people watching from all around the world. She sang the aria in her own unique way. She blended styles of music as she had done so many times before. She was a little afraid that opera fans would not like her version. She did not need to worry. The audience stood up to applaud. After that, Aretha received invitations to sing classical pieces with orchestras around the nation.

On February 26, 1997, Aretha posed for photos at the 39th annual Grammy Awards in New York City. She was performing and presenting at the ceremony.

On April 10, 2001, Aretha gave a concert at New York's Radio City Music Hall. She performed the live, televised concert for VH1's Divas Live: The One and Only Aretha Franklin.

Aretha long had been a queen. She became a diva two months after the Grammy Awards. A diva is a famous and dramatic female singer. In 1997 VH1 invited Aretha to perform on *VH1 Divas Live*. VH-1's *Diva* shows focus on successful female singers. The producers paired the 56-year-old singer with a group of much younger artists. They included Mariah Carey, Shania Twain, and Celine Dion.

In April of 2001, VH1 created a special program to honor Aretha. "VH1 Divas Live: The One and Only Aretha Franklin" was entirely about Aretha and her music. She sang her trademark **soul** and **gospel** numbers as well as **jazz,** opera, and classical songs. She even joined rapper Kid Rock for a **hip-hop** song. Her son Teddy played guitar and sang background vocals. The show was filmed at the world-famous Radio City Music Hall in New York City.

Branching out

Aretha frequently uses her amazing voice to help raise money for good causes. The VH1 *Divas* concerts are held for charity. She has sung at a benefit for the Rosa and Raymond Parks Foundation. Rosa Parks is called the mother of the **Civil Rights Movement.** In 1956, she refused to give up her seat on a bus for a white rider in a Montgomery, Alabama. That act led to a **boycott** of the Montgomery bus system. The boycott lasted until the bus company ended **segregation** on its buses.

Aretha has shown that she can adapt her style to any kind of music. Here, Aretha performed a hip-hop song with rapper Kid Rock at the live, televised concert for VH1's Divas Live: The One and Only Aretha Franklin.

Aretha also loaned her musical talents to the Jackie Robinson Foundation. Robinson was the first African American to play major league baseball. Both the Parks and the Robinson charities help people of color.

Aretha has not limited her energies to music, however. She loves to cook and is working on a book of classic soul food recipes. Soul food is a traditional, black way of cooking that blends the foods of Africa and the American South. Aretha also dreams of opening a chain of restaurants in the Detroit area. She plans to call them Aretha's Chicken and Waffles. She would also like to make a film biography of Mahalia Jackson.

Aretha's dreams may take her back to Hollywood and Los Angeles occasionally. However, she does not want to live there again. She much prefers the Detroit area. She says she likes the community feeling of the city of which she is a key member. The Queen of Soul regularly holds parties in Detroit. She also attends her father's old church and performs solos there on occasion.

Aretha's **gospel** roots have taken her far. Her love for them also has brought her back.

Glossary

arrange to change a piece of music someone else has performed so that it can be played on different instruments, in a different way

blues type of structured emotional, sometimes sad music first sung by African-American slaves.

boycott to refuse to buy or take part in something as a way of protest

Chitlin Circuit collection of nightclubs, hotels, and concert halls that hosted African-American performers

civil rights personal freedoms guaranteed to all Americans under the Constitution of the United States

Civil Rights Movement organized struggle to gain full citizenship rights for African Americans. It took place during the 1960s.

color bar a barrier preventing African Americans from participating with whites in various activities

congregation group of people collected together to worship

cover in music, a song that was originally written and recorded by another performer

equal rights when people have the same opportunities and are treated the same, regardless of their race or gender

gospel music based on religious songs of praise. Gospel combines traditional church songs with African-American musical styles.

hip-hop urban movement that began in the 1970s that combined a style of dancing, art, music, and dress. It became popular through break dancing, graffiti art, and rap music. Hip-hop music usually refers to a type of music that features elements of rap music, pop, and R & B. It doesn't necessarily have to be spoken, or rapped.

jazz lively music that is full of rhythm. It was invented by African Americans in the early 1900s.

lyric words of a song

producer person in charge of making a record

race riots outbreaks of violence between blacks and whites

racism practice of the belief that one race is better than another

reputation what other people have heard about a person

rhythm and blues (R & B) music that mixes the sound of blues with African-American folk music and a strong beat

segregation separation of blacks and whites according to law

sharecropping working another person's land in return for a share of the crop

single song off an album that is released separately for radio play

soul style of music blending rhythm and blues and gospel

Timeline

1942: Aretha is born on March 25 in Memphis, Tennessee

1944: The Franklins moves to Detroit. Reverend Franklin becomes minister of New Bethel Baptist Church

1954: Aretha begins singing in the church choir.

1956: Aretha records her first **gospel** album.

1966: Aretha signs a contract with Atlantic Records.

1967: "Respect" hits number one on the charts.

1967–1974: Aretha wins the Grammy Award for Best Female R & B Vocal Performance seven years in a row.

1968: Aretha sings at the funeral of **civil rights** leader Dr. Martin Luther King Jr.

1972: Aretha wins a Grammy Award for Best **Soul** Gospel Performance on Amazing Grace.

1976: Aretha records the soundtrack for the movie *Sparkle.*

1977: Aretha sings at the inaugural celebration of President Jimmy Carter.

1980: Aretha acts and sings "Think" in *The Blues Brothers* movie.

1981: Aretha wins a Grammy Award for Best Female R & B Vocal Performance.

1985: Aretha wins Grammy Awards for Best Female R & B Vocal Performance and Best R & B Song.

1987: Aretha becomes the first woman in the Rock and Roll Hall of Fame and wins two more Grammy Awards.

1988: Aretha wins a Grammy Award for Best Soul Gospel Performance, Female—Singles, Albums, or Tracks.

1993: Aretha sings at the inaugural celebration of President Bill Clinton.

1994: Aretha receives Grammy's Lifetime Achievement Award.

1998: Aretha appears in the *Blues Brothers 2000* movie.

2001: VH1 honors Aretha in "VH1 Divas Live: The One and Only Aretha Franklin."

Further Information

Further reading

Flanders, Julian, Ed. *The Story of Music: Gospel, Blues, and Jazz. Volume 5.* Danbury, Conn: Grolier Educational, 2001.

Grimbly, Shona, Ed. T*he Story of Music: From Rock and Pop to Hip-Hop. Volume 6.* Danbury, Conn.: Grolier Educational, 2001.

Vernell, Marjorie. *Leaders of Black Civil Rights.* Farmington, Mich.:Gale Group, 2000.

McAvoy, Jim. *Aretha Franklin.* Philadelphia, Penn.: Chelsea House, 2002.

Addresses

Rock and Roll Hall of Fame and Museum
1 Key Plaza
751 Erieside Avenue
Cleveland, OH 44114
Write here to learn more about Aretha's election into the Rock and Roll Hall of Fame.

Center for American Music
University of Texas at Austin
School of Music
1 University Station, E3100
Austin, TX 78712
Write here to learn more about American music and its roots.

Center for Black Music Research
Columbia College
600 South Michigan Avenue
Chicago, IL 60605
This center specializes in black music from all around the world. Write here for more information about African-American music.

Index